Voice

Nicola Edwards

EVANS BROTHERS LIMITED

Save the Children

Published by Evans Brothers Limited in association with Save the Children UK

© 2004 Evans Brothers Ltd and the Save the Children Fund

Evans Brothers Limited
2A Portman Mansions
Chiltern Street
London W1U 6NR

First published 2004

British Library Cataloguing in
Publication Data
Edwards, Nicola
Voice. – (Children's rights)
    1. Freedom of speech - Juvenile literature
    2. Children's rights - Juvenile literature
    I. Title
    323.2'52

ISBN 0 237 525542

Printed in China

Credits:
Series editor: Louise John
Editor: Patience Coster
Designer: Simon Borrough
Production: Jenny Mulvanny

Acknowledgements
Cover and title page: Kalpesh Lathigra
p6: Neil Cooper/Jan Hammond
p7: Kalpesh Lathigra
p8: Tim Hetherington
p9: Tim Hetherington/Network
p10: Tim Hetherington/Network
p11a: Tim Hetherington/Network
p11b: Tim Hetherington/Network
p12a: Kalpesh Lathigra
p12b: Dan White
p13: Tim Hetherington/Network
p14: Tim Hetherington/Network
p15: Tim Hetherington/Network
p16a: Stuart Freedman/Network
p16b: Kalpesh Lathigra
p17: Dario Mitidieri
p18: Michael Amendolia/Network
p19a: Michael Amendolia/Network
p19b: Michael Amendolia/Network
p20: Kalpesh Lathigra
p21: Simon Wood
p22: Kalpesh Lathigra
p23a: Kalpesh Lathigra
p23b: Kalpesh Lathigra
p24: Dan White
p25a: Michael Amendolia/Network
p25b: Kalpesh Lathigra
p26: Michael Amendolia/Network
p27a: Michael Amendolia/Network
p27b: Michael Amendolia/Network

Contents

All children have rights

The history of rights for children   In 1919, a remarkable woman called Eglantyne Jebb founded the Save the Children Fund. She wanted to help children who were dying of hunger as a result of the First World War. Four years later, she wrote a very special set of statements, a list of children's rights. Eglantyne Jebb said that her aim was "to claim certain rights for children, and labour for their universal recognition". This meant that she wanted worldwide agreement on children's rights.

It was many years before countries around the world agreed that children have rights, but eventually the statements became recognised in international law in 1989. They are known as the United Nations Convention on the Rights of the Child (UNCRC). The rights in the UNCRC are based on the idea that everyone deserves fair treatment.

The UNCRC is a very important document. Almost every country in the world has signed it, so it relates to most of the world's children. The rights listed in the UNCRC cover all areas of children's lives such as their right to have a home and their right to be educated.

Children have a right to be involved in decisions that affect their lives. These children in Mali, Africa, are taking part in a discussion about their rights.

Children meet at this club in Nepal to discuss their experiences and share ideas about how their lives could be improved.

Rights for all?

The UNCRC should mean that the rights of children everywhere are guaranteed. However, this is not the case. Every day, millions of children are denied their rights. Children suffer discrimination because they are poor, or disabled, or because they work for a living. It might be because of their religion, race or whether they are a boy or a girl.

Children are very vulnerable, so they need special care and protection. The UNCRC exists to try to make sure that they are protected.

The right to a voice

Several of the Articles in the UNCRC are about every child's right to speak out and be listened to. Knowing they have the right to a voice can make children feel confident about expressing their opinions and discussing with others things that are important to them. Here are some of the Articles:

Article 12 You have the right to an opinion, especially about things that affect you, and for your views to be listened to and taken seriously.

Article 13 You have the right to find out about things and express your ideas, through making art, speaking and writing, unless this breaks the rights of others.

Article 15 You have the right to meet with friends and join or set up clubs, unless this breaks the rights of others.

Article 42 Children and adults need to be told about children's rights.

Save the Children

Save the Children UK is part of the International Save the Children Alliance working in over 100 countries worldwide to make children's rights a reality. This book and the others in the series tell the stories of children around the world who are achieving their rights with the help of Save the Children projects.

Children have the right to be involved

Taking part Every day, children take part in the world around them, in their homes, schools and communities. They form opinions about things that happen to them. They often wish that some parts of their lives could be different. They may have hopes and dreams for the future.

By getting involved and playing an active part in their world, children can help to improve things. For example, in some developing countries, where many people are very poor, millions of children die every year from diseases such as measles and tuberculosis. These diseases can often be prevented by vaccination, but many parents do not know that they can have their children vaccinated.

Aid workers have trained children like Ali to spread the news in their communities about how vaccination can protect children against disease. You can read Ali's story on pages 10 and 11.

Spreading the word

Children can make a big difference to one another's lives. They can pass important information between themselves in ways they can understand. For example, children are

"I want to help people in my village."
Ali, 15, Burkina Faso, West Africa.

Children in Ethiopia put on a puppet show to teach others what they have learned about HIV and AIDS.

helping one another learn about HIV and AIDS (Acquired Immune Deficiency Syndrome). In some countries, many children are at risk of being affected by HIV/AIDS because they do not have information about it. The HIV virus is spread when blood or other body fluids from an infected person mix with another person's. The virus attacks the body and stops it fighting off any disease. HIV causes AIDS, an illness for which there is no cure at the moment.

In countries such as Nepal and Peru, children have been trained to become peer educators. This means they teach other children about the HIV virus and explain how to avoid getting it.

Teaching one another

Wherever children live, receiving a good education is crucial to their development. But millions of children around the world do not get an education. This may be because they are poor, disabled, or a refugee. Two out of every three children who do not have the chance to go to school are girls. Without an education, it is hard to find a good job and escape from poverty. In some communities, children have become mentors to others, helping them to learn and develop their skills.

Seventeen-year-old Yadav (left) dropped out of school because his teachers could not cope with his deafness. After struggling to get an education, he is now a mentor for other disabled children in Nepal, helping them receive a good education.

Ali's story

Ali, who is 15, lives in northern Burkina Faso in West Africa. He knows his village, Titabé, very well. This is because he walks for miles around it every Thursday and Saturday afternoon. Ali visits families and encourages the parents to take their children to be vaccinated. Through vaccination, the children will be protected against diseases such as tuberculosis, diphtheria, tetanus, whooping cough, polio, measles and yellow fever.

Ali is a volunteer for a project that advises families of the benefits of vaccination. In the two years since the project began, Ali has visited hundreds of families. His involvement in his community has made a big difference to the health of children in the village. Ali says, "I volunteered because I know that if I encourage people to go to the vaccination sessions, they will be protected from disease and they will be in good health."

The project began when a team from Save the Children visited Ali's school and asked the children to tell them about any problems in the village. The children said that very few parents were taking their children to the health centre to be vaccinated. The team asked volunteers from the school to find out which children

Ali checks the list of children in his village who need to be vaccinated.

needed to be vaccinated. The volunteers went around the village gathering information. Soon the notebooks they had been given were filled with names.

The team then trained Ali and the other volunteers so that they could explain to parents why their children should be vaccinated. They could also tell them where the free vaccination sessions were taking place. Ali has found that the children often listen to him more closely than they do to their parents. He explains, "When we go into a family, the whole family is there, and the children listen particularly well to us. I'm sure that if it were an adult talking, they wouldn't listen as well. When an adult is talking, children can't come close. But when we talk, they come closer because we're their friends, and they know that we're there for them. And if there are things that the children don't understand, they can ask us to explain more."

Ali and other volunteers spread the news about vaccination to parents and children. Ali says: "If the parents don't listen, the kids usually do."

Ali says he has grown in confidence since becoming involved in the project. He's proud of what he has achieved by taking part in it. He says, "All the children who have been to the vaccination sessions are protected, and none of them have had the diseases. So now when I go to families, they all listen to me carefully."

Ali has found that children feel comfortable listening to him because he is a child too.

Children have the right to make decisions about their future

Fighting prejudice   Children have the right to be involved in the decisions that are made about their lives. But many children throughout the world are not given opportunities to fulfil their potential. Some children are denied the chance to say what they would like from life because they are disabled.

In many developing countries, disabled children have to struggle to achieve their right to a good education. In Nepal, Sangita, who is blind, had to take a test to prove she was bright enough to be allowed into school. Then she had to fight for her right to take an exam, because she needed a Braille exam paper. She is proud of her achievements and now she encourages other disabled children to follow her example.

Sangita would like to become a teacher when she is older.

These children live on the streets in Vietnam. A project has been set up to offer them education and healthcare and give them the chance to enjoy themselves.

Fighting poverty

Often the biggest barrier to children growing up healthy, happy and well-educated is the fact that they are living in poverty. Some children leave home to look for ways of earning money because their families cannot afford to care for them. With nowhere to live, they often end up sleeping on the streets of a city. At 'drop-in centres' in countries such as Tajikistan, street children can get advice and medical help. They can attend courses which will help them begin to make better lives for themselves. Mirzovali, aged 17, says the children he meets at the centre are like his family, and they help one another. At the centre, he says, children "can understand about their future, learn something, get a vocation."

Fighting injustice

Some children have terrible experiences in their early lives, which they need help to overcome. In a number of developing countries, such as the Democratic Republic of Congo, young children fight as soldiers. When they leave the army, many of these children find it very hard to settle back into their communities and their future can look bleak. Some benefit from projects that help former child soldiers earn money to support themselves and their families. Putting the past behind them, they are able to work towards a more hopeful future.

Tonton used to be a soldier. Now he is training to be a mechanic. He has paid for his training out of the money he earns by breeding rabbits for food.

"If I go to school, I think I'll have a better future. It would be like a guarantee for my life." Tonton, 17, Democratic Republic of Congo.

13

Djike, Jirèse and Dieu's story

Djike (left), Dieu (middle) and Jirèse (right) in their street-cleaning overalls.

"Over here!" yelled Jirèse, sprinting down the wing. He could see the goalkeeper was off his line. Skilfully, Dieu passed the ball to Jirèse, who ran past a defender and then booted the ball as hard as he could. "Goal!" shouted Djike, running over to hug his brother.

Djike is 11, a year younger than Jirèse. Their friend, Dieu, is 14. All three boys are members of the same football club. Through the club, they have become involved in a project supported by Save the Children which has helped them to make a big difference to their lives.

The boys live in a poor and overcrowded area of Kinshasa, the capital city of the Democratic Republic of Congo. With little money coming in, life is a struggle. Their fathers are unable to find work and their mothers buy and sell what they can. Until recently, it looked as though the boys would have to leave school because their parents could not afford the fees. Then the boys had an idea. Dieu explains: "We said, let's look for something to help ourselves."

One day at the football club, they heard about a local street-cleaning project. Members of football clubs in the area are paid to collect rubbish from the streets and the market place. Then the rubbish is sorted into different types. The items collected which do not rot, such as bottles and plastic bags, are sold to market traders. Items that do rot, such as fruit and vegetables swept up from the market, are sold as garden compost. The compost is used to grow vegetables in the gardens of the football clubs. Djike, Jirèse and Dieu decided to join the project because they realised it would be a way of earning money to pay for their school fees.

As Dieu says, "I work here because the money they pay me is my money. I can use it the way I want." The boys also work in the gardens, and take home a share of the vegetables.

Djike says, "I like working in the garden. It's like being trained. One day I might have my own garden. So even if I don't have a job, I'll at least know how to grow things in a garden."

Their cleaning work made such a difference to the streets that the boys suggested to project members that they should clean the places where they live as well. Jirèse says, "When you live in a clean environment you won't get sick. It makes it a better place to live." Dieu agrees: "Children can make big changes. They can suggest things that are very important to change a situation."

The children collect rubbish from the streets and sort it into piles for selling or recycling.

15

Children have the right to speak out

Making a difference   There is an old saying: "Children should be seen and not heard." But, throughout the world today, children are showing how they can make a difference to their lives by speaking out about things they think are wrong and unfair.

Fifteen-year-old Jorge (right), who was born blind, has his own radio show in Honduras. He says, "The most important thing for young people is to express themselves."

Children have a right to express their views. But many children are afraid to do so because they are worried that they will be ignored or not taken seriously. It is difficult to feel confident when you are poor and your rights are continually being denied. It takes courage to speak out. But children who have done so find that their confidence has grown, and they can change things for the better.

Children are the future

Children have a right to talk about their experiences and express their opinions about what

These children in Nepal are making a video to communicate their opinions and ideas to other people.

DID YOU KNOW?

In the world today, 20 million children have been forced to leave their homes because of war.

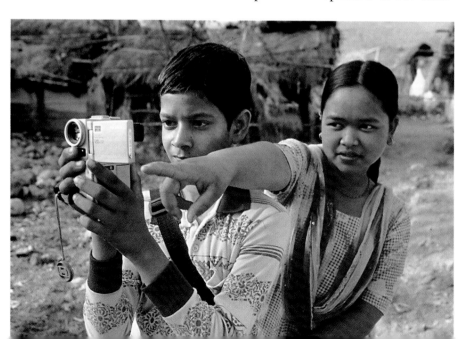

"We have to raise our voices so that other children won't be exploited and denied their rights." Sangita, 17, Nepal.

happens in the world in which they are growing up. For example, they may want to protest against their country going to war or damaging the environment.

Speaking out can take different forms. Some children sign petitions or go on marches as a way of making their opinions heard; others make speeches. Some use the Internet to speak out. Through the Internet, children can find out what daily life is like for other children who are living in the middle of conflict. For example, groups of Palestinian children living in refugee camps have described their experiences on a website. You can visit their website at www.savethechildren.org.uk/eyetoeye.

These girls are members of a children's parliament in Rajasthan, India.

Taking part Children often gain confidence from one another. They get together and talk about what changes they would like to see in their local areas and in the wider world.

In some schools, children have set up councils so that they can have their say in how the school is run. Pupils in the school vote to decide who will become a councillor. The councillors then put forward the views of the pupils they represent. If children have the chance to say what they would change about the world they live in, they can help to improve the lives of other people.

17

Maria Alejandra's story

Eleven-year-old Maria Alejandra lives with her parents and younger sister and brother in Medellin, Colombia. The family do not have a lot of money, but Maria Alejandra does not consider herself to be poor. She says, "To me, poverty means suffering, being humiliated and not being healthy. Thankfully I haven't experienced that myself."

For Maria Alejandra, the problem that affects her and thousands of others in her city is violence. In the last ten years in Medellin, about 50,000 people have been killed. Many of these killings were the result of arguments about drugs or money, or involved rival gangs fighting for control of different areas of the city. This atmosphere of violence spilled over into the city's classrooms. Children began taking weapons to school, and fighting each other in the playground. Maria Alejandra says, "I think there are so many people fighting

in my community because they don't know how to talk to each other – they just kill people and they need to learn how to communicate instead."

Maria Alejandra in the playground at her school.

18

Maria Alejandra says, "I like being with my friends and sharing with them."

Learning how to communicate is exactly what has been happening at Maria Alejandra's school. This is because the children there have become involved in a project called 'Living Together'. The project encourages tolerance and respect for others. In a recent election campaign to become the leader of the 'Living Together' representatives in the school, Maria Alejandra spoke out about how she thought life at school could be improved. She said, "My proposals were to make the school nice and clean, to solve conflicts, to have entertainment and activities, like visiting the best park in Medellin, and to play micro-football and basketball."

The children agreed with her, and she won the election. She says, "The other pupils liked what I said and voted for me like when they elected the president of Colombia. It made me feel very happy."

As a 'Living Together' representative, Maria Alejandra helps to solve conflicts between children at the school. She encourages them to discuss their differences, rather than using fights to settle arguments. Everyone has noticed a change in the children's behaviour. Maria Alejandra says, "There used to be lots of fighting in our school, but then we got very excited about improving things. Before, we weren't motivated to change anything, but now all the classes are competing to be the best."

Taking part in the project has made Maria Alejandra feel happy and confident. Speaking out has given her hope for the future. She says, "Before I became a representative I used to be very serious and I didn't like being with the other children much because I felt afraid of them. Now I participate in activities in the classroom and get others involved too. Starting with us, things can change outside in our community too."

Break times at school are much more relaxed as a result of the 'Living Together' project.

19

Children have the right to be heard

The need to listen   Adults can make decisions that improve children's lives. To make the right decisions, adults need to listen to what children have to say. Children can explain what life is like for them – they can talk about the good things and the things that could be improved. Children often feel strongly that something is unfair and needs to change. It is sometimes difficult for adults to hear and accept that they have got things wrong. But children need to be involved in the decisions affecting their lives.

Changing people's minds   In some countries, such as Nepal, girls are treated very unfairly. Their opinions are not considered to be important, and they are often denied their right to an education. Sometimes they cannot even walk around their local area without being shouted at or followed. Experiences like this can make girls feel lonely and unhappy.

By joining a group, girls can talk to others who have had similar experiences. Once the girls discover they are not alone, they can support

As a result of asking children to talk about how their lives could be improved, literacy classes have been set up for these children in Nepal.

DID YOU KNOW?
Currently, about 110 million of the world's children are being denied their right to a primary school education. Over half of these children are girls.

one another and challenge what is happening to them. Members of some children's groups in Nepal have talked to the adults in their local area about the problems they face. The adults have listened to them, and changed their attitudes towards the girls as a result.

Improving lives

Children can make changes to their lives by collecting information from one another and passing it on to adults. Surveys carried out by children have revealed how many children are missing out on healthcare or education. As a result, children's lives have improved. Vaccination programmes have been set up to protect children from disease. Laws have been changed to make sure disabled children get an education to suit their needs. In some countries, special classes have been organised so that children can learn to read and write and develop their skills in maths. With good education and healthcare, children can build better lives for themselves.

Making their feelings known: children in a refugee camp in Liberia wave placards to draw attention to their demands.

"If adults understand children's feelings, they can help them to achieve their dreams." Tika, 16, Nepal.

Dilmaya's story

Dilmaya is a leading member of her children's group.

Dilmaya sighed as she looked at the huge pile of stones in front of her. It was late afternoon and time for her to start work, even though she had only just returned home from school. Dilmaya's stomach rumbled. She'd had nothing to eat since the breakfast she had cooked for her mum and herself at 9 a.m. that morning.

Still, thought Dilmaya, if she could break stones for the next two hours, she would have enough to sell to the local building contractor. It would earn her about 180 rupees (around £1.70) – enough to buy lentils and rice. There might even be money left over for some new stationery. And at least she had her friends to chat to as she worked. Dilmaya enjoyed being with her friends. She couldn't wait until the weekend, when they all would meet at the local children's club.

Around 20 children belong to the club, which is situated in the mid-western region of Nepal. The children meet regularly to discuss issues that concern them. Then they talk to adults such as politicians, who listen to their views. The children take part in activities to raise awareness of important issues in the community. Dilmaya is the secretary of her group. She says, "I have to write up the discussion and share it with all the group members. I enjoy this role very much."

The children in the group put together and perform plays to communicate their message to other people. They act out their ideas for the changes that they would like to see in their local community. Dilmaya explains: "We made up a story about unfair treatment of step-daughters. We chose this because it's happening in this village and other villages. We performed this play in the community. I think they realised they shouldn't discriminate between daughters and step-daughters. All children are the same."

The children have grown in confidence as they have learnt to organise their meetings and speak out about issues that concern them. They can raise these issues by performing in plays or taking part in discussions with adults in a child welfare committee meeting. For the children in Dilmaya's group, one of the most satisfying results of their work is that adults now listen to them. Dilmaya says, "If children work together, they get the respect and trust of parents, other relatives and neighbours. If anything bad happens to any child, we can speak up about it and make sure that it doesn't happen in the future."

Dilmaya (third from the left) and her friends, collecting stones they have broken. The stones will be sold to a local building contractor.

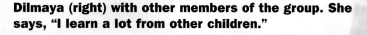

Dilmaya (right) with other members of the group. She says, "I learn a lot from other children."

23

Children have the right to know about their rights

Rights and wrongs

All children have the right to grow up in a good home where they are safe, looked after by people who care about them. They have the right to an education and to healthcare. But some children in the world are denied these rights. Poverty is the main reason for this. Children living in poverty may not even know they have these rights at all.

The problems of poverty

If a family is poor, everyone in the family becomes involved in the struggle to survive. If a poor child is disabled, the family may not be able to pay for the care that he or she needs. If it is necessary to pay for education, then poor children will not be able to go to school. Instead they may have to help out at home, with housework or by looking after younger brothers and sisters.

"When children know their rights, they know how to speak up when they see something that's wrong."

Dennis, 12, Honduras.

Children have to work in difficult and dangerous conditions in this factory in Bangladesh.

DID YOU KNOW?

At the moment there are more than 200 million working children under the age of 14. These children are often employed in conditions that put their health and safety at risk.

Girls whose lives have been affected by violence can learn about their rights at this drop-in centre in the Philippines.

Some children from poor families go out to work to earn money. They may be badly treated by employers, and made to work long hours for very little pay. Some children leave home to find work and end up living on the streets, in unhealthy and often dangerous conditions. Others have to leave their homes because of conflict, and live in temporary camps as refugees until it is safe for them to return. Sometimes children become separated from their families and must cope on their own.

Teenage girls run these night classes for the children of a village in Nepal.

Helping children

Projects have been set up to help children learn about their rights. Knowing that they have rights, and that they can help to change their lives for the better, gives children confidence and makes them feel happier. Some projects help working children and street children discover that they have rights. These projects also help children achieve their rights. They provide after-work classes in subjects which help the children in their daily lives. Learning maths, for example, can help children avoid being cheated by the people who buy the things they make.

Verônica's story

Verônica lives with her parents and six brothers and sisters in a poor area of Recife, in north-eastern Brazil. The family's house has three bedrooms, and when everyone is at home it can feel very crowded. Verônica's father is unemployed and her mother earns a little money by washing clothes for people.

When she was 12 years old, Verônica left school and went out to work to earn money for her family. Six years later she feels sad looking back at the things she missed out on because she was working: "I don't think it's right for children to work as hard as I have during the last six years. At 12, the best of your life begins – it's a time for you to enjoy and think about what you want to do later in life. You shouldn't have to sacrifice your happiness at that age."

Verônica is a domestic worker, which means that she works in a house, keeping it clean for the people who live there. This is how she describes her day: "I start at 7:30 a.m. and go home whenever I finish, which is normally around 3 p.m. I get a break to have lunch and a snack. I wash clothes by hand, wash the dishes, sweep and mop the

Knowing about her rights has helped Verônica. She says, "My mind is more open now, it's made me feel important."

floor, clean the furniture and the bathrooms and do the ironing. There are four people in the family, so there are a lot of clothes to wash."

When Verônica was 16, a survey was carried out among 200 girls working in Recife. The survey was part of a project to find out about the living and working conditions of domestic workers. As a result of the survey, the project members set up workshops. They used song, dance, drama and discussions to make domestic workers aware of

Verônica (in the centre at the back) was one of the 39 girls and one boy who attended workshops for young domestic workers.

their rights – as children and as workers. Verônica says the workshops have made a big difference to her life: "I've seen that there are other girls who are doing the same work, some even younger than me. When you first come here you feel embarrassed talking about your job, but when you've discussed it and you've learned things, you're not embarrassed to talk to other girls any more and say: 'Listen, you don't have to accept that – that's not right!'"

Verônica has now become a 'multiplier' for the project. This means she passes on what she has learned to other domestic workers. With

At the workshops, girls can have fun and learn about their rights.

new confidence, she has gone back to school to catch up on the education she missed. In the future she aims to get a better paid, more interesting job. Meanwhile, she is helping to put together a book to teach girls about their rights. She says, "I feel happy about continuing with the project. If I couldn't come here any more there'd be an empty space in my life because it's very good for my mind, and the affection we receive here makes us feel really good."

Glossary

AIDS Acquired Immune Deficiency Syndrome: AIDS is caused by a virus which attacks the body's immune system and stops it fighting off disease.

article A part of a legal document, such as a convention.

Braille A system of writing which uses raised dots that blind people can read by touch.

children's rights The rights that everyone under the age of 18 should have, including the right to life, the right to food, clothes and a place to live, the right to education and health, and the right to be protected from danger.

community The group of people who live in an area.

conflict A serious disagreement between two or more groups of people which can lead to fighting.

developing countries Countries that have few industries and in which many people are very poor.

disabled When part of the body does not work properly. Sometimes children are born with a disability or it may be the result of an accident. Disabilities can be physical (to do with the body) or mental (to do with the mind).

discrimination The unfair treatment of a person because of their race, religion or whether they are a boy or a girl.

founded A word meaning started.

healthcare A service which offers treatment to people who are ill and which promotes ways of living healthily.

HIV Human Immunodeficiency Virus: the virus that leads to AIDS.

mentor Someone who gives help and guidance to another person, usually younger than themselves.

peer educators Children who teach what they have learned to others the same age.

prejudice A negative opinion of someone, based on looks, behaviour, race, religion etc. rather than on fact.

projects Schemes that are set up to improve life for local people.

refugee camps Camps where people who have had to leave their homes can live, usually for a short time, until it is safe for them to return.

refugees People who leave their home country because they feel unsafe.

street children Children who are homeless and live on the streets of a city rather than with their families.

tuberculosis An infectious disease which affects the lungs.

United Nations An organisation made up of many different countries that was set up in 1945 to promote international peace and cooperation.

vaccination Injecting a person with the safe form of a disease. Vaccination enables the person's body to fight off the disease in the future.

vocation The sort of work a person feels drawn to do.

volunteer Someone who gives their time without being paid for what they do.

Index

Further reading and addresses

Books to read

Save the Children (*Taking Action* series), Heinemann Library/
Save the Children, 2000

Stand Up, Speak Out, Two-Can Publishing, 2001

Packs for teachers

Partners in Rights (a photo pack using creative arts to explore
rights and citizenship for 7-14 year olds), Save the Children,
2000

A Time for Rights (explores citizenship and rights in relation to
the UN Convention on the Rights of the Child, for 9-13 year
olds), Save the Children/UNICEF 2002

Young Citizens (a pack looking at the lives of five young citizens
around the world, for Key Stage 2), Save the Children, 2002

There is a summary version of the UN Convention on the
Rights of the Child at www.childrensrights.ie/yourrights.php

Useful addresses

Save the Children
1 St John's Lane
London EC1
www.savethechildren.org.uk

UNICEF UK
Africa House
64-78 Kingsway
London WC2B 6NB
www.unicef.org

Save the Children Australia
Level 3
20 Council St
Hawthorn East
Vic 3123
www.savethechildren.org.au

UNICEF Australia
Level 3
303 Pitt St
Sydney
NSW 2000
www.unicef.com.au